Stone Circles *in* Ireland

Seán Ó Nualláin

Country House, Dublin

Published in 1995 by
Town House and Country House
Trinity House
Charleston Road
Ranelagh, Dublin 6
Ireland

British Library Cataloguing in Publication Data. A catalogue record for this book is available from the British Library.

ISBN: 0-946172-45-5

Illustration acknowledgements
Vincent Steadman, map of sites, page iv; Office of Public Works (copyright), photos 1, 2, 3, 4, 5, 6, 7, 8, 11; Archaeological Branch, Ordnance Survey Office, photos 9, 10, 12, 13, 14, 15, 16; Anthony Weir, plate 3; Michael Herity, plate 4; Liam Blake, plate 7 (cover). All the other plates are by Seán Ó Nualláin.

Cover: *Stone circle at Drombeg, Co Cork*

Series editor: Michael Ryan
Text editor: Elaine Campion
Design & artwork: Bill and Tina Murphy
Colour origination: The Kulor Centre
Printed in Ireland by ßetaprint

CONTENTS

Newgrange and the eastern circles   6

The Ulster series   13

The western circles   16

The Cork–Kerry series   35

The function of the circles   44

Glossary   46
Select bibliography   47
Index   48

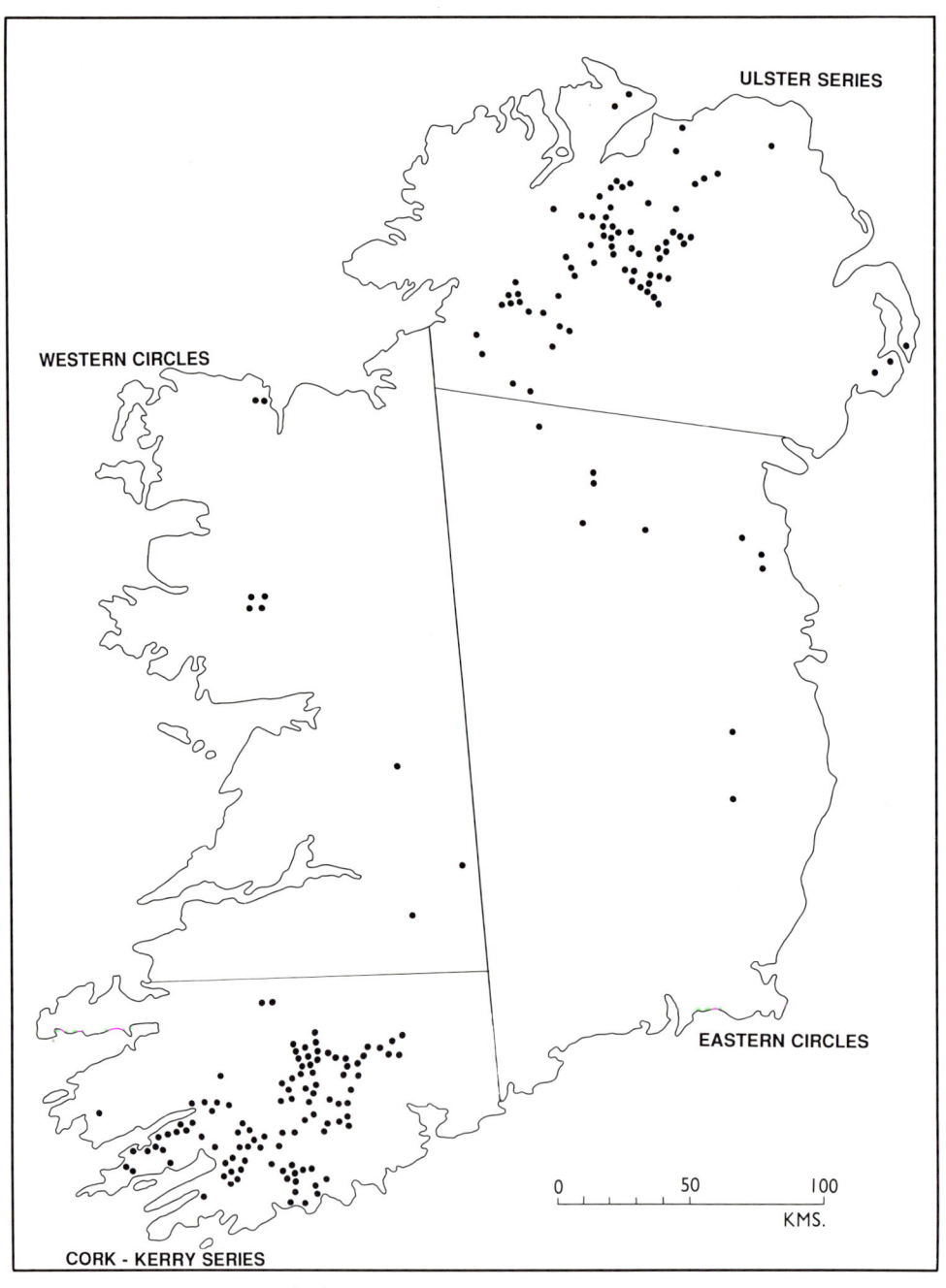

ULSTER SERIES

WESTERN CIRCLES

EASTERN CIRCLES

CORK - KERRY SERIES

0   50   100

KMS.

Distribution of stone circles in Ireland

Few prehistoric monuments in Ireland or Great Britain have inspired as much interest or speculation as the circles of upright stones, of which that surrounding the famous passage-tomb at Newgrange, County Meath, is the best known Irish example. Stone circles consist essentially of various forms of circular or near circular enclosures built of stones, set apart rather than contiguously, and dedicated to ceremonial or ritual practices. The stones are of megalithic proportions and the areas enclosed can vary from as little as 3m in diameter to 50m, or even more in exceptional cases. Some individual circles seem to be aligned on the rising or setting sun or moon at the summer or winter solstices, but whether or not this was intentional is open to question. However, at some homogeneous groups of circles it is clear that their builders were content to set the main axes of their monuments within a broad band centred on a north-east/south-west axis.

While the nature of the activities that took place in or around the circles must inevitably remain obscure, the human remains recovered from excavated examples indicate that many circles must have been intimately connected with death and burial.

Radiocarbon dating suggests that the majority of Irish and British stone circles were erected during the Bronze Age which, in Ireland, may have lasted for over fourteen hundred years, from about 2100 BC to about 700 BC. However, finds of Neolithic pottery and stone artefacts at a minority of excavated monuments point to earlier activity at some of the sites.

Stone circles frequently enclose or are accompanied by other classes of monument or are themselves surrounded by a bank or fosse or both. In Ireland, the circles may contain stone-built burial structures, monoliths and, in a few cases, passage-tombs. Outside the circles, though nearby, there may be monoliths, pairs of stones, long or short stone rows, boulder-burials or cairns. Apart from boulder-burials, the British circles have somewhat similar associations, though long stone avenues, unknown in Ireland, and internal burial cairns also occur. Some British stone circles are set within large embanked   *5* enclosures known as henges, which derive their name from the famous site of Stonehenge, on Salisbury plain in Wiltshire, where the initial phase is represented by a circular bank with an external fosse. Unlike Stonehenge, the normal henges have internal fosses and the areas enclosed can vary from 17m to 110m in diameter, or considerably more in a few cases. Henge-type monuments are rare in Ireland, though there is a group of thirteen embanked enclosures near the Boyne, Nanny and Delvin River valleys in County Meath which are thought to be related to them. Some of these Meath examples bear a close spatial relationship to local passage-tombs. There are a few similar enclosures elsewhere in Ireland, the most notable being that at Ballynahatty, County Down, which has, close to its centre, the roofed chamber of a small passage-tomb. Henges are generally considered to have been ritual centres or perhaps places of assembly and were constructed in the Late Neolithic period, about 2300 BC.

Over two hundred and forty stone circles are known in Ireland. The majority of these occur in two major concentrations, a mid-Ulster group consisting of an estimated one hundred and ten circles, most of which are in Counties Tyrone, Derry and east Fermanagh, and a south Munster series of one hundred and seven examples which occupy large areas of Cork and south-west Kerry. Between these are eighteen widely dispersed circles, ten on the eastern side of the country, extending from Wicklow to Cavan, and the other eight stretching from Lough Gur in County Limerick to the north coast of County Mayo.

NEWGRANGE AND THE EASTERN CIRCLES

Foremost among the eastern sites is the circle of spaced, upright stones surrounding the huge cairn that covers the principal Newgrange passage-tomb (Photo 1, Pl 1). Only twelve stones survive out of an estimated total of thirty-five. The circle is 103.6m in average diameter and is the largest stone circle in Ireland. The cairn, apple-shaped in plan and 85m in maximum dimension,

Photo 1 *The site at Newgrange, Co Meath, before excavation. The four large stones in front of the entrance to the passage-tomb are part of a circle of an estimated thirty-five monoliths placed around the mound in the Early Bronze Age. The stones vary from 1.8m to 2.4m in height.*

incorporates a 19m-long passage leading to a large cruciform chamber which is covered by an elaborate corbelled roof some 6m in height. Many of the stones of the tomb, passage and surrounding kerb are decorated and display some of the finest megalithic art in Atlantic Europe.

The Newgrange tomb was built in the Neolithic period, probably about 3000 BC. Centuries later, incoming Beaker-using people, probably from Britain, constructed a large pit-and-post circle some 27m to the east of the tomb entrance, and the northern perimeter of this came as close as 8m to the kerb of the cairn. This circle, which may have been up to 100m in external diameter, consisted of three concentric rows of pits, with post-holes on the inside. The circle has been dated to around 2000 BC, though its precise function is not known. Excavation has also shown that the great stone circle is later than the 7 pit-and-post monument and is associated with a second phase of Beaker settlement on the site. It would seem likely, therefore, that the Newgrange stone circle was one of the earliest of such monuments in Ireland. The juxtaposition of the two monuments, and their comparable diameters, suggest that at least some stone circles owe their origins to timber prototypes.

Several other stone circles in this north Leinster region and in east County Cavan are associated with passage-tombs. In the mid eighteenth century, an antiquary named Thomas Wright published plans and drawings of two adjacent hilltop passage-tombs at Killin Hill, County Louth, some 25km to the south-east of Newgrange. The larger of these, on the main hilltop, was surrounded by a circle of upright stones and bore 'rude carvings' similar to Newgrange. A single stone with megalithic ornament is all that now survives on the site. The second monument may also have stood within a stone circle, but this is not altogether clear from the early accounts. No trace of this example remains.

The major passage-tomb cemetery on the Slieve na Calliagh hills lies some 40km to the west-north-west of Newgrange in the same county. About 1km to the north of the summit of Carnbane East is the remains of a large stone circle situated on gently undulating land in Ballinvalley townland. While the circle has no direct association with the overlooking passage-tombs, its presence here may well be significant. Four erect and five prostrate stones on the site represent a circle about 29m in diameter. The erect stones vary from 1.5m to 2.5m in height. Two further stones, set in line, indicate an entrance passage, 4.5m long, at the north-west. Five or six monoliths extend northwards over a distance of 0.8km from the site, but the relationship of these to the circle is not clear.

Two little-known stone circles are situated on a platform on the lower slopes of Slieve Glah, an isolated hill some 6km to the south-east of Cavan town. Nearby are two round Bronze Age barrows and a circular earthen enclosure of uncertain affinities. The larger of the two stone circles is about 40m in diameter and is represented by five erect and seven prostrate stones. The five upright stones are 0.65m to 1.3m in height. Within the circle is the base of an oval cairn measuring 25m by 22m. Protruding from this are a number of stones that seem to represent a kerb some 17m in diameter. Several small set stones towards the south-east may mark the position of a megalithic chamber. It would seem probable that a passage-tomb stood here, and this likelihood is enhanced by the presence within the cairn of a loose stone bearing what seems to be megalithic art. The remains of the second stone circle stand about 30m to the north of the first circle. Here seven set stones rise at intervals from the inside of a low semicircular bank, 3.5m wide and 50cm high. The two tallest stones rise 80cm and 30cm above the bank.

Another County Cavan circle is situated on a hillock about 3.8km south-west of the village of Ballyconnell, in Killycluggin townland, where seven erect and five or six fallen stones delimit an area about 21m in diameter. Two long pillar-like stones at the north-eastern part of the perimeter are parallel to each other and seem to form an entrance passage. A small test-cutting of an area 1m wide and 3m in length within the circle produced no archaeological evidence.

The last of the circles in this northern group is situated 2.5km east-north-east of the town of Granard in the townland of Cartronbore, County Longford. Nine stones mark the perimeter of this circle, but all save two of these have fallen. The area enclosed was about 20m in diameter.

The distribution of the eight circles described above suggests that they were erected by independent communities, each with its own ritual or ceremonial monuments. It would seem likely, however, that the groups who placed their circles around passage-tombs shared certain beliefs about their predecessors.

Apart from the circle at Beltany, County Donegal, and a possible destroyed example at Moydam in north Antrim, stone circles enclosing passage-tombs are not known elsewhere in Ireland. Such associations are rare across the Irish Sea also, though there is a remarkable group at Clava, to the south of Moray Firth in north-east Scotland, where stone circles surround a number of simple passage-tombs and related ring-cairns. There is also an isolated, though spectacular, example at Callanish, on the island of Harris and Lewis in the Outer Hebrides.

9

Here the small two-chambered passage-tomb and its cairn are surrounded by a circle of exceptionally tall, thin slabs, which itself stands at the middle of a cruciform arrangement of stone avenues and rows, composed, again, of tall stones. There are no known connections between these monuments and the Irish examples.

In the southern part of this eastern region, earlier workers listed ten monuments in Counties Wicklow and Kildare as stone circles, but of these only two, both in Wicklow, are accepted as true examples. The stone circle at Athgreany, known as 'The Piper's Stones', is situated on a hill-terrace to the east of the Castledermot road, some 8km south-south-east of Kilcullen village (Photo 2). Twelve stones of the circle survive, but only five of these are in their original positions. These erect stones indicate that the circle had been about 23m in diameter. An outlying boulder some 40m downhill to the north-east seems to

Photo 2 *Ruined stone circle at Athgreany, Co Wicklow.*

be a glacial erratic and is not necessarily associated with the circle. Grooves on
its upper surface and similar grooves on one of the fallen circle-stones may have
been caused by the weathering of quartz veins.

The second Wicklow circle, at Boleycarrigeen, lies about 6km to the east of
Baltinglass village (Photo 3, Pl 2). It stands on a hill-platform in a forest
clearing and is difficult to find without a guide. The stones here are set at the
inner face of a low 1m-wide bank. Eleven of an estimated total of seventeen
stones survive, and these are thin, narrow slabs which contrast markedly with
the rounded granite boulders employed at the Athgreany circle. Two stones at
the north-east, one 1.8m tall and the other somewhat lower, mark the entrance.
The stone diametrically opposed to these is the lowest stone in the circle, and
the other orthostats decrease in height as they approach this stone. This grading
in height is a characteristic feature of the Cork–Kerry circles and it is quite

Photo 3 *Embanked stone circle at Boleycarrigeen, Co Wicklow. The pointed stones in the
middle of the picture flank the entrance to the circle. The commanding position of the
monument is now obscured by a surrounding forest.*

11

possible that the builders of the Boleycarrigeen circle were related to those who erected the southern circles.

Another Wicklow monument, at Castleruddery, is sometimes taken to be a stone circle but is actually an embanked enclosure (Photo 4). This lies 7.5km to the north-east of Baltinglass and is 1km east of the Ballymore Eustace road. The circular bank here, with an interior and exterior facing of stones, encloses an area about 30m in diameter. Two massive quartz boulders on the eastern part of the perimeter flank the entrance. Air photography has revealed the presence of a concentric cropmark a considerable distance outside the enclosure, which may indicate the presence of a fosse.

12   Photo 4 *Quartz conglomerates flanking the entrance to the embanked enclosure at Castleruddery, Co Wicklow.*

THE ULSTER SERIES

The mid-Ulster stone circles are largely concentrated in County Tyrone, on the plateau south of the Sperrin Mountains, with smaller outlying examples in the neighbouring counties of Derry, Fermanagh and Donegal. Unlike stone circles elsewhere, these Ulster circles are usually composed of quite small stones, few over 50cm in height, though stones up to 1m high are present at some examples. The circles often occur as clusters and can be accompanied by long and short stone rows, monoliths and small kerbed burial cairns. Many sites are enveloped in the blanket-peat bogs of the region, their presence signalled by the protrusion of a few of the taller stones of an underlying circle or row. Thus, what can be said of the complex as a whole, has to be based on the few sites that have been scientifically excavated as well as those that have been otherwise denuded.

The most informative excavation to date took place at Beaghmore, 13.5km to the west-north-west of Cookstown in County Tyrone (Pl 3). The group of monuments uncovered here extends over an area measuring 145m by 55m, but their full extent is not known. Up to 2m of peat covers the surrounding area. The structures now visible consist of three pairs of irregular-shaped circles, eight stone rows, some composed of tall stones aligned north-east south-west, and twelve small kerbed cairns, most of which contained a cremation burial. One of the cairns stood within a circular bank with an internal fosse. Here also and close together are two stone rings, each surrounding a multitude of small upright stones, few over 10cm in height, which form no obvious patterns. An earlier phase on the site is represented by four bands of tumbled stones, which seem to be fallen field-fences. Stone circles are notoriously poor in datable finds, and Beaghmore is no exception in this regard. Two hearth pits yielded sherds of five Neolithic vessels, one of the cairns produced a porcellanite axe and a number of crude flint implements, and flint flakes were found in or on the mineral soil beneath the blanket peat. Radiocarbon dating indicates that the circles, rows and cairns were erected within a time bracket of 1535 and 775 BC, in Late Bronze

13

Age times, and that the Neolithic activity on the site commenced about 3300 BC.

Meagre finds have been reported from two other excavated sites. The complex at Drumskinny, 7.25km north-north-east of Kesh in County Fermanagh, consists of a stone circle, a cairn and a stone row. The circle was originally composed of thirty-nine spaced upright stones, 30cm to 1.8m in height, which enclosed an area 13m in diameter. The cairn, which stands 1m from the north-western part of the perimeter, was carefully constructed and was contained within a kerb almost 4m in diameter. Stretching southwards from the cairn, for a distance of 15m, is the row, which originally consisted of twenty-four small upright stones. A crude hollow-scraper and a few worked flints were found under and around the cairn, but there was no evidence for burial. The only other find was a sherd of Neolithic pottery from the old ground level near one of the stones of the circle. This and the hollow-scraper do not necessarily date the monuments to the Neolithic period. The second site is at Cuilbane, 3.5km south-south-west of Garvagh in County Derry. Here, during restoration work at a very ruined stone circle, the excavator recovered a cache of Neolithic flint implements from the packing around one of the stones of the circle. He was satisfied that this provided secure evidence for the construction of at least some of the Ulster circles during the Neolithic period.

On Copney Hill, 6km to the north-north-west of Carrickmore village in County Tyrone, is a complex which first came to archaeological notice in 1979. At that time the complex was seen to consist of stone circles, a stone row and a solitary tall monolith. Though still partly covered in blanket bog, it was clear that the site was best compared with the Beaghmore group, 11.25km to the north-east.

A unique association occurs at Clogherny, about 3km north of Plumbridge village in County Tyrone. Here an excavated wedge-tomb and its cairn are surrounded by a circle of seventeen well-spaced upright stones standing about 1m high and set in a rough paving.

14   There are three circles in north County Donegal that are not of the mid-Ulster type. One, known as the Bocan circle, lies 1.75km south-east of Culdaff village. Here seven stones, 1–2m high, indicate a circle some 20m in diameter. The second, at Carrowreagh, 5.5km south-east of Carndonagh, is largely covered by bog. Six orthostats represent a circle that may be 26m in diameter. About 125m to the east is a wedge-tomb, also partially exposed in the bog. The third circle is on the summit of Tops Hill, 2.5km south of Raphoe, and lies 3.2km to the north-west of the Kilmonaster passage-tomb cemetery. The great circle here is represented by sixty-four stones of an estimated eighty and encloses an area some 45m in diameter. The stones average 1.2m in height, though a massive slab at the south-west reaches the imposing height of 2.75m. Within the circle is the base of a cairn which may have contained a passage-tomb. A monolith 1.8m high stands 21m away to the south-east. An Iron Age Celtic carved stone head was found within the circle.

On the east coast, near the mouth of Strangford Lough, are three unusual Ulster circles. That on Castlemahon Mountain, 4.4km south-west of Strangford, consisted originally of six orthostats, about 1m high, enclosing an area 21m in diameter. Excavation near one of the stones revealed a small pit containing charcoal, worked flints and sherds of Neolithic bowls. Near the centre of the circle was a large pit in which a fierce fire had burned, and beside this was a tiny cist containing the burnt bones of a child and a Neolithic flint knife.

At Ballynoe, 4km south of Downpatrick, is a circle of over fifty stones, up to 1.8m high, enclosing an area 35m in diameter. Within is a long cairn containing, at the west, a segmented gallery of Scottish type and, at the east, a cist. A ring of stones enclosed the eastern end of the cairn. The recovery of a sherd of Carrowkeel ware (passage-tomb pottery) and the presence of baetyls (small smooth stones) indicates passage-tomb affinities.

A site at Millin Bay on the Ards peninsula has even stronger passage-tomb associations. Excavation of a mound here showed that the earliest feature present was a dry stone wall. Beside this was a burial chamber 5.5m long and less than 1m wide containing the bones of at least fifteen individuals. An oval

15

ring of flagstones surrounded the chamber and many of these were decorated with art akin to that of the passage-tombs. Further links with these tombs is indicated by Carrowkeel ware and baetyls and the presence of eleven monoliths which surrounded the covering mound.

THE WESTERN CIRCLES

The more southerly of these circles is at Lough Gur, County Limerick. The fertile limestone land here attracted settlement from Neolithic times onwards and is rich in prehistoric monuments. There are many stone rings in the area, the remains of habitation enclosures and ritual monuments, but only one true stone circle (Photo 5, Pl 4). This stands a short distance to the north-west of the

16 Photo 5 *Stone circle at Grange, Lough Gur, Co Limerick. The low circular mound within the circle is covered by weeds.*

cont. p 32

Pl 1 *The entrance to the Neolithic passage-tomb at Newgrange, Co Meath. The monoliths in the foreground form part of the great stone circle placed around the tomb in Early Bronze Age times.*

17

Pl 2 *Embanked stone circle at Boleycarrigeen, Co Wicklow. The ranging pole stands between the entrance stones, opposite the lowest stone of the circle. This example is clearly a derivative of the multiple-stone circles of Cork and Kerry.*

Pl 3 *Part of the complex of stone circles, burial cairns and stone rows at Beaghmore, Co Tyrone. The stones exposed in the foreground represent the base of an earlier Neolithic fence.*

(Facing page)
Pl 4 *Stone circle and great enclosure at Grange, Lough Gur, Co Limerick. The bank of the enclosure is 9m in width and the area enclosed is 45m in diameter. The inner face of the bank is lined with contiguous stones. The entrance passage can be seen at the top right-hand side of the bank.*

18

Pl 5 *Stone circle at Bauraglanna, Co Tipperary. This example is in the Rearcross-Silvermines district, where there is reason to believe that local copper ores may have been mined in the Early Bronze Age.*

20

Pl 6 *Nymphsfield stone circle, near Cong, Co Mayo. Thirteen of the twenty-one spaced stones here are set in the inner face of a low bank. The stones are well-spaced, flat-topped limestone slabs.*

Pl 7 *Stone circle at Drombeg, Co Cork. This is the best known and most accessible circle in Co Cork. Nearby are the foundations of two circular huts and an ancient cooking place known as a Fulacht Fiadh.*

Pl 8 *The top surface of the axial stone at the Drombeg, Co Cork, stone circle. The line-carving here is reminiscent of the shape of a stone axe. It is 30cm in length and 18cm in maximum width and surrounds a circular hollow. Nearby is a second hollow. The date and significance of the carving are unknown.*

22

Pl 9 *Five-stone circle at Carrigagulla, Co Cork. This circle is now enclosed by a State forest, but is on display to the public. The small axial stone is an unusual feature.*

Pl 10 *Boulder-burial within the stone circle at Kenmare, Co Kerry. Small pad-stones, like that to the right of the picture, are sometimes used by the builders of such monuments to steady the cover-stone above its supports.*

24

Pl 11 *Stone circle at Gortanimill, Co Cork. Within this circle can be seen the stump of a quartz monolith.*

Pl 12 *Monuments at Kealkil, Co Cork. The complex here consists of a five-stone circle, a pair of standing stones and, in the foreground, a cairn with radially-set stones on its perimeter. Excavations produced no dating evidence or artefacts at any of the monuments.*

Pl 13 *A radial-stone cairn at Knocknakilla, Co Cork. The cairn here is accompanied by a pair of monoliths, one fallen, and a ruined five-stone circle (Photo 13).*

Pl 14 *Five-stone circle and monolith at Uragh, Co Kerry. Situated between Cloonee Lough Upper and Lough Inchiquin, the circle is of the five-stone type but one of the entrance stones has fallen. The monolith, 3.10m high, is set just 60cm in front of the axial stone.*

Pl 15 *Stone row at Farrannahinney, Co Cork. This is an elegant example of a Cork–Kerry type stone row. One of the stones has fallen. The other four are graded in height, with the tallest stone at the south-west. These monuments sometimes accompany five-stone circles.*

28

Pl 16 *Stone row at Killadangan, Co Mayo. The row here is of Cork–Kerry type. It consists of five stones, one of which has fallen, and is aligned north-east south-west. Three monoliths can be seen in the middle ground towards Croagh Patrick.*

cont. from p 16

massive enclosure known as the Lios. The circle is composed of fifteen stones, up to 1.4m high, enclosing an area 16m in diameter. There is a 30cm-high mound within the circle and a slight bank has been observed beyond the perimeter.

The next example is 34km north-east of Lough Gur, on the slopes of Keeper Hill in County Tipperary. The site is in Bauraglanna, 4km south of Silvermines village (Pl 5). Here eleven erect stones suggest a circle 12.5m in diameter. The tallest stone is 2m in height, the others are less than 1m high, and the tops of some are broken. Five low upright stones beyond the perimeter are of uncertain significance.

The third of these circles is at Commons East in south-west Galway and is 2.15km to the north-north-west of Woodford village. The site is on a boggy ridge about 150m north-east of the Loughrea road. Seven quite small stones here define a circle almost 11m in diameter. The stones are symmetrically arranged and are graded in height. The tallest stones, which mark the entrance, are at the north-east, and opposite these is the lowest stone of the group. The circle is clearly a relative of the Cork–Kerry series.

The remaining five circles are all in County Mayo. Three of these form a cluster about 3km to the north-east of Cong village, and with them is the remains of an embanked enclosure. These rings stand in a limestone district rich in burial cairns and other prehistoric monuments which, in the last century, was erroneously identified as the site of the first Battle of Magh Tuireadh, described in early Irish mythology. They lie to the east of the Ballinrobe road, opposite an old rectory, and are within 90m to 180m of each other.

The northern circle of the cluster is enclosed by a fence (Photo 6). Thirty stones, some broken, represent a circle 16m in diameter, which encloses a mound 4m across and 30cm high. The stones are 20cm to 1.25m in height and some are set contiguously. The circle to the south-west of the last is also surrounded by a fence (Pl 6). Twenty-one stones here, up to 1.2m in height, indicate a circle 17.5m in diameter. Thirteen of the stones are set into the inner

Photo 6 *Stone circle in Glebe, near Cong, Co Mayo. As can be seen in the picture, some of the stones are set contiguously. The trees to the left stand on a low mound, 4m in diameter, but this is not necessarily an ancient feature.*

base of a low earthen bank. The eastern circle is represented by ten erect and six fallen stones. The erect stones are up to 1m in height and surround an area measuring 14.5m by 19m (Photo 7).

The stone enclosure lies to the south of the circles (Photo 8). Eighteen

Photo 7 *Stone circle in Tonaleeaun, near Cong, Co Mayo.*

33

upright stones, set on the inner and outer faces of an earthen bank, form a segment of a ring which seems to have been about 32m in diameter. The stones do not exceed 1.45m in height.

There is one extant stone circle and the site of another on the north coast of Mayo, about 4km to the north of Killala. The former, at Rathfran, consists of sixteen stones, five of which are prostrate. The erect stones, 50cm to 1.6m in height, stand in a low bank and indicate a diameter of about 18m. The second circle, in Rathfranpark, stood within a few metres of a wedge-tomb. It was removed soon after 1951 and the debris from it dumped on one end of the tomb.

(Facing page)
Photo 8 *Part of the enclosure in Nymphsfield, near Cong, Co Mayo. The picture shows the earthen bank, flanked on both sides by erect stones. The form of construction here is reminiscent of that at Castleruddery, Co Wicklow (Photo 4).*

THE CORK–KERRY SERIES

The Cork–Kerry stone circles form part of a great concentration of interrelated free-standing megalithic monuments, cairns and enclosures. These include two hundred short stone rows of two to six stones, over six hundred monoliths, eighty-seven boulder-burials and eighteen cairns or enclosures distinguished by the radially-set stones marking their perimeter. The stone circles are frequently accompanied by one or more of these monuments and sometimes enclose boulder-burials or monoliths.

The Cork–Kerry circles form a remarkably homogeneous group, conforming to standard concepts of design and orientation. They are composed of an uneven number of stones, symmetrically arranged, with an axial stone on the south-western section of the perimeter, standing opposite the entrance. A characteristic feature of the circles is the decrease in the heights of the stones from the entrance down to the axial stone. The circles fall into two categories: five-stone circles and multiple-stone circles. Apart from the number of stones involved and their greater diameters, the multiple-stone examples differ from the others in their shape, in the occasional elaboration of their entrances and in the types and dispositions of the monuments associated with them.

35

(Facing page – Top)
Photo 9 *Stone circle at Dromroe, Co Kerry. At the centre of the circle stands a boulder-burial, and 2m to the south of this is a flat-topped monolith, also within the circle.*

(Facing page – Bottom)
Photo 10 *A well preserved, free-standing boulder-burial at Bawngare, Co Cork. The cover-stone here is 2.9m long, 1.9m wide and up to 1m thick.*

The fifty-two multiple-stone circles are delimited by stones ranging from seven to nineteen in number (Pl 7). Most are close to circular in outline, but a notable exception is the egg-shaped circle on the outskirts of Kenmare town. Maximum internal measurements are from about 4m in the few with seven stones to 17m at Kenmare, which seems to have had fifteen stones. The commonest form of entrance is marked by two perimeter stones opposite the axial stone, and these are distinguished only by their height. In others the entrance stones are set end-on to the circumference, and in three of these, two additional stones serve to form an elongated entrance passage. The axial stone, unlike the other stones, is usually set with its longest axis on the perimeter. Its top is frequently flat and level, but examples with marked internal slopes also occur (Pl 8).

Few of the fifty-five five-stone circles are circular in outline and most tend to be D-shaped. with the vertical line of the D representing the axial stone (Pl 9). The areas enclosed are small in comparison with those in the multiple-stone examples, their main axes ranging from 2.3m to 4m. The entrance stones are frequently set with their long axes approaching each other towards the east, but in two instances they stand end on to the other three stones to form a short passage. Unlike those in the larger circles, the axial stone is seldom the longest stone on the perimeter. Again the top of this stone may be flat and level or have an internal sloping surface, but in a few instances it is quite small and has a pointed top.

Both varieties of circle may have outlying monoliths or pairs of standing stones, while the five-stone examples alone may be accompanied by rows of three or four stones, cairns, enclosures or combinations of these monuments (Photos 12–14, Pls 12–15). Unlike the smaller examples, multiple-stone circles can sometimes contain or be accompanied by monoliths or boulder-burials and a few are surrounded by a bank or a bank and fosse (Pls 9–11, Photo 15).

36

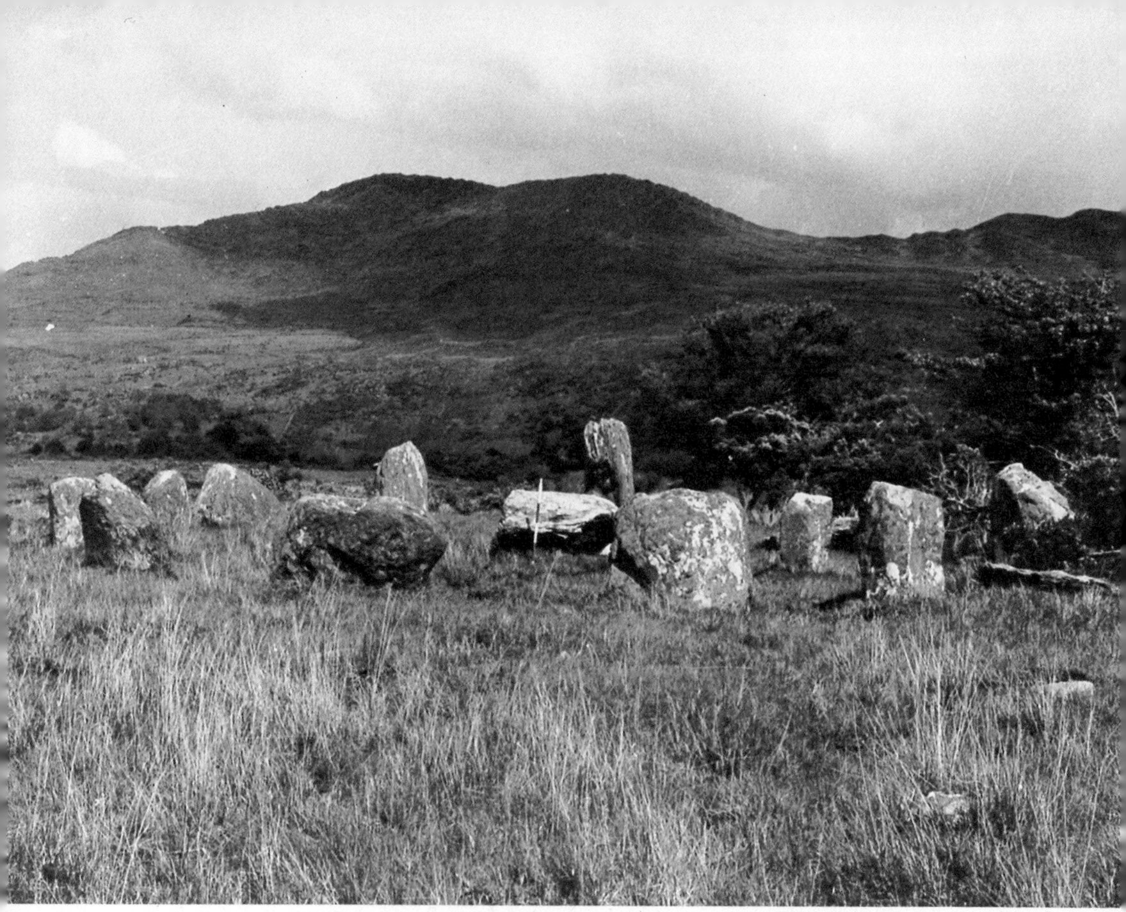

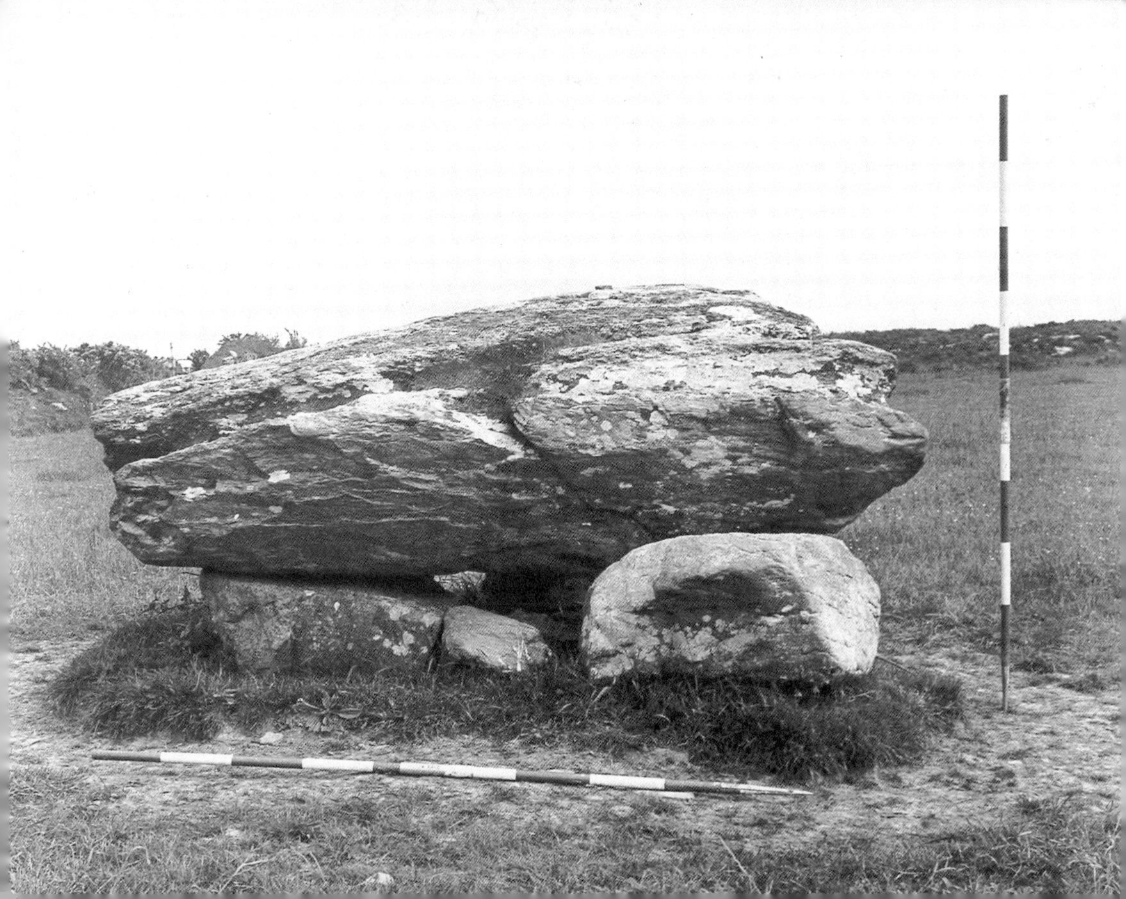

Photo 11 *Five-stone circle at Knocknaneirk, Co Cork. The horizontal ranging-pole rests on a natural ledge on the axial stone. The vertical pole, 2m in height, stands between the entrance stones. The measurement along the main axis of the circle is 3.85m and the greatest width is 3.05m.*

Photo 12 *The complex at Knocknakilla, Co Cork. The monuments here include a ruined five-stone circle, a small cairn with radially-set stones on its perimeter (Pl 13), and a pair of monoliths, one of which is now prostrate. Excavation at the circle produced no finds but uncovered a great number of white quartz stones.*

38

Photo 13 *Five-stone circle and stone row at Cabragh, Co Cork. One stone of the circle seems to be missing and two others are incorporated in the fence crossing the monuments. The four massive stones of the row extend over a distance of 7.9m. The stones are aligned north-east south-west and are graded in height. The tallest, at the north-east, is 3.3m in height.*

Photo 14 *A small five-stone circle and attendant monolith at Maughanaclea, Co Cork. The monolith here is about 2m in height.*

39

Photo 15 *Embanked stone circle at Lissyviggeen, Co Kerry. The circle of seven stones here encloses an area about 4m in diameter. It is surrounded by an earthen bank, up to 2m in height and 3m to 5m in width. The area enclosed is 20m in diameter. A pair of outlying stones stand 11.5m to the south of the bank. They are 2.2m apart and are 1.7m and 2.35m in height.*

40

Photo 16 *Stone circle at Drombeg, Co Cork. On 24 December 1957 and again on 23 December 1958, the setting sun was observed along the main axis of the circle. It was found that the sun sank below the horizon at a point to the south of the V-shaped gap in the hills.*

Orientation

The main axis of a Cork–Kerry type stone circle is manifestly a line extending from the middle of the gap between the entrance stones across the centre of the axial stone, dividing the monument into two roughly symmetrical parts. The axes can be reliably established in sixty-five cases. A plot of the directions of these shows that when viewed from the entrance, the axes all fall within a band lying between south and west-north-west. It also emerges that within the splay of 107° present, there is clear bias towards the south-west. The axes of the stone rows and pairs throughout Cork and Kerry present a pattern akin to that of the circles. Thus, the circles, rows and pairs are so built that their axes indicate a general alignment on the sectors of the heavens in which the sun rises and sets, and both series tend to group in a north-east/south-west band, pointing to a winter rather than a summer position for the sun (Photo 16).

Excavations

Four of the six excavated circles produced evidence for burial. The three multiple-stone examples, Drombeg, Bohonagh and Reanascreena, all in County Cork, each had central pits, the former two containing cremated bone. The small central pit at Reanascreena contained soil only, but a second pit there contained some minute pieces of cremated bone. The five-stone circle at Cashelkeelty, County Kerry, enclosed a pit, covered by a slab, which held cremated remains thought to be those of an individual aged 25–30 years. The evidence suggests that individual cremation burials, in pits, are to be expected in Cork–Kerry stone circles. Among unexcavated examples, the occurrence of boulder-burials in eight or perhaps nine circles must surely signal the presence of similar interments.

The burial at Drombeg was that of a young adolescent and was contained in a pot set upright in the pit. This coarse flat-bottomed vessel is of uncertain date. Among the finds from the Cashelkeelty five-stone circle and its accompanying stone row were two flint arrowheads, one leaf-shaped and the other barbed and tanged, a convex scraper, also of flint, and a portion of a sandstone object thought to be an ard point. The arrowheads link the site with the Late Neolithic/Early Bronze Age period, but two radiocarbon dates from the circle suggest that it was erected during the period 970–715 BC. These dates are supported by dates of 945 BC and 830 BC from Drombeg. Dates from charcoal deposits near two stone rows, at Dromatouk, County Kerry, and Maughanasilly, County Cork, suggest that these were built several centuries earlier than the stone circles.

Distribution and economy

Apart from one or, perhaps, two examples in County Galway, stone circles of the Cork–Kerry type are not known elsewhere in Ireland or Great Britain. They occupy three main regions: the highlands flanking the basin of the River Lee, the rolling lowlands east of Clonakilty, and the fringes of the Beara peninsula. No general custom of siting is evident, though examples on hill slopes are frequently found on small natural platforms, which interrupt the general gradient of the ground. The multiple-stone sites are found throughout the distribution but predominate in coastal regions, as do the boulder-burials. Few of the five-stone circles are near the coast and only two lie below the 100m contour.

The general upland distribution of the circles, with over seventy-seven per cent situated above 100m, indicates a preference for thin, well-drained soils suitable for cattle husbandry. Cereal cultivation was also practised, as is shown by the analysis of peat monoliths from the vicinity of the circles at Cashelkeelty, which identified cereal pollen considered to be contemporary with the construction of the monuments.

A further aspect of the circle-builder's economy seems to be implied by the presence of monuments near the copper deposits at Bantry, Kenmare and Killarney and on the Beara peninsula. Boulder-burials, stone rows and monoliths also show a widespread association with the copper-bearing areas. There is no direct evidence that the builders of these monuments had an interest in the copper but, given that the Mount Gabriel mines in County Cork were in use between 1700 BC and 1300 BC, it is possible that some did. The presence of quartz monoliths within some stone circles may suggest that this was so. Quartz is an indicator of some forms of copper (and gold) ore and if, as seems likely, prehistoric copper-seeking peoples were aware of this association, it may well explain the special status accorded to these quartz monoliths. Direct association of the earlier wedge-tombs with copper is suggested by the discovery of a decorated bronze axe and two fragments of raw copper at the entrance to a wedge-tomb at Toormore on the Mizen peninsula.

THE FUNCTION OF THE CIRCLES

The use or uses of stone circles can never be fully understood. Since over a thousand circles of various forms are known in Ireland and Great Britain, built over a period of perhaps fourteen hundred years, a uniformity of function is hardly to be expected. There is, for instance, an obvious distinction between those associated with human burial and others which are not. The former predominate and occur mainly in northern and western Britain and Ireland. The others, for the most part, are in southern Britain, and some of these may have been used as places of assembly for secular purposes. The builders of many of the circles with funerary associations, especially those in Cork and Kerry and a related series in Aberdeenshire, placed the main axes of their monuments in the north-eastern and south-western quadrants of the horizon. This emphasis on the sectors of the heavens in which the sun rises and sets suggests that the builders of these circles may have regarded the sun as a symbol of death and rebirth.

Ard point: the scratching component of a primitive light plough.

Barrow: an artificial mound of earth covering one or more prehistoric burials.

Beaker folk: people who used a distinctive form of flat-based pottery at the beginning of the Bronze Age in Ireland, *c* 2000 BC.

Boulder-burial: a boulder, up to 3.35m in maximum dimension, resting on three or more low stones, above a shallow pit containing a cremated burial.

Cairn: a heap of stones containing one or more burial structures.

Cropmark: where buried features such as ditches or walls affect the covering soil and alter the colour of grass or other crops. Ditches are indicated by dark lines while walls appear as lighter bands of parched vegetation.

Fosse: a ditch

Megalithic: built of large stones.

Monolith: a single standing stone.

Neolithic: pertaining to the New Stone Age, *c* 4000 BC to *c* 2500 BC, when agriculture and cattle husbandry was developed in Ireland.

Passage-tomb: a megalithic tomb consisting of a circular mound surrounded by a kerb and enclosing a passage leading to a burial chamber. The structural stones frequently bear carved or pocked designs.

Post-hole: a pit containing a timber post.

Radiocarbon dating: a method of dating based on the measurement of the rate of decay of a radioactive isotope (carbon-14), which occurs in all organic material.

Ring-cairn: a round cairn with a kerb and a concentric inner ring of stones enclosing an open area.

Wedge-tomb: a megalithic tomb consisting of a long burial chamber, often with a short portico or antechamber at the western end and, occasionally, a small end chamber at the east. The tomb is usually wider and higher at the west and is frequently enclosed in a wedge-shaped cairn.

SELECT BIBLIOGRAPHY

Burl, Aubrey, *The Stone Circles of the British Isles*, Yale University Press, New Haven and London, 1976.

From Carnac to Callanish, The Prehistoric Stone Rows and Avenues of Britain, Ireland and Brittany, Yale University Press, New Haven and London, 1993.

Chart, DA (ed), *A Preliminary Survey of the Ancient Monuments of Northern Ireland*, HMSO, Belfast, 1940.

Ó Nualláin, Seán, 'Boulder-burials', *Proceedings of the Royal Irish Academy*, vol 78C (1978), 75–114.

'A survey of stone circles in Cork and Kerry', *Proceedings of the Royal Irish Academy*, vol 84C (1984), 1–77.

'Stone rows in the south of Ireland', *Proceedings of the Royal Irish Academy*, vol 88C (1988), 179–256.

INDEX

References to illustrations are in *italics*.

Aberdeenshire, Scotland, 45
Ards peninsula, Co Down, 15
Athgreany ('Piper's Stones'), Co Wicklow, 10, *10*, 11

Ballinvalley, Co Meath, 8
Ballyconnell, Co Cavan, 9
Ballynahatty, Co Down, 6
Ballynoe, Co Down, 15
Baltinglass, Co Wicklow, 11, 12
Bantry, Co Cork, 44
Bauraglanna, Co Tipperary, *20*, 32
Bawngare, Co Cork, *37*
Beaghmore, Co Tyrone, 13, 14, *18*
Beara peninsula, 43, 44
Beltany, Co Donegal, 9
Bocan circle, Co Donegal, 15
Bohanagh, Co Cork, 43
Boleycarrigeen, Co Wicklow, 11–12, *11*, *18*
Boyne, River, 6

Cabragh, Co Cork, *39*
Callanish, Harris and Lewis, Outer Hebrides, 9
Carnbane East, *see* Slieve na Calliagh
Carndonagh, Co Donegal, 15
Carrickmore, Co Tyrone, 14
Carrigagulla, Co Cork, *23*
Carrowreagh, Co Donegal, 15
Cartronbore, Co Longford, 9
Cashelkeelty, Co Kerry, 43, 44
Castlemahon Mountain, Co Down, 15
Castleruddery, Co Wicklow, 12, *12*, 35
Clava, Moray Firth, Scotland, 9
Clogherny, Co Tyrone, 14
Clonakilty, Co Cork, 43
Cloonee Lough Upper, Co Kerry, 27
Commons East, Co Galway, 32
Cong, Co Mayo, 21, 32, 33, 35
Cookstown, Co Tyrone, 13
Copney Hill, Co Tyrone, 14
Croagh Patrick, Co Mayo, 30
Cuilbane, Co Derry, 14
Culdaff, Co Donegal, 15

Delvin, River, 6
Downpatrick, Co Down, 15
Dromatouk, Co Kerry, 43
Drombeg, Co Cork, *21*, *22*, *42*, 43
Dromroe, Co Kerry, *37*
Drumskinny, Co Fermanagh, 14

Farrannahinney, Co Cork, *28–9*

Gabriel, Mount, Co Cork, 44

Garvagh, Co Derry, 14
Glebe, Co Mayo, *33*
Gortanimill, Co Cork, *26*
Granard, Co Longford, 9
Grange, Lough Gur, Co Limerick, *16*, *19*

Kealkil, Co Cork, *26*
Keeper Hill, Co Tipperary, 32
Kenmare, Co Kerry, *24–5*, 44
Kesh, Co Fermanagh, 14
Kilcullen, Co Wicklow, 10
Killadangan, Co Mayo, *30–1*
Killala, Co Mayo, 35
Killarney, Co Kerry, 44
Killin Hill, Co Louth, 8
Killycluggin, Co Cavan, 9
Kilmonaster, Co Donegal, 15
Knocknakilla, Co Cork, *27*, *38*
Knocknaneirk, Co Cork, *38*

Lee, River, 43
Lios, the, Co Limerick, 32
Lissyviggeen, Co Kerry, *40–41*
Loughcrew hills, *see* Slieve na Calliagh
Lough Gur, Co Limerick, 6, 16, 18, 32
Lough Inchiquin, Co Kerry, 27

Maughanaclea, Co Cork, *39*
Maughanasilly, Co Cork, 43
Millin Bay, Co Down, 15–16
Mizen peninsula, Co Cork, 44
Moydam, Co Antrim, 9

Nanny, River, 6
Newgrange, Co Meath, 5, 6–8, *7*, *17*
Nymphsfield, Co Mayo, *21*, *34*

Plumbridge, Co Tyrone, 14

Raphoe, Co Donegal, 15
Rathfran, Co Mayo, 35
Reanascreena, Co Cork, 43

Silvermines, Co Tipperary, 32
Slieve Glah, Co Cavan, 8–9
Slieve na Calliagh, Co Meath, 8
Sperrin Mountains, Co Tyrone, 13
Stonehenge, Salisbury, England, 6
Strangford Lough, Co Down, 15

Tonaleeaun, Co Mayo, *33*
Toormore, Co Cork, 44
Tops Hill, Co Donegal, 15

Uragh, Co Kerry, *27*

Woodford, Co Galway, 32
Wright, Thomas, 8